ALMOST HOME

Words and Music by BART MILLARD,
MIKE SCHEUCHZER, NATHAN COCHRAN,
ROBBY SHAFFER, BARRY GRAUL
and BEN GLOVER

Moderately, in 2

PIANO · VOCAL · GUITAR

TOP CHRISTIAN HITS OF
2019-2020

20 POWERFUL SONGS

ISBN 978-1-5400-8510-8

Visit Hal Leonard Online at
www.halleonard.com

Contact us:
Hal Leonard
7777 West Bluemound Road
Milwaukee, WI 53213
Email: info@halleonard.com

In Europe, contact:
Hal Leonard Europe Limited
42 Wigmore Street
Marylebone, London, W1U 2RN
Email: info@halleonardeurope.com

In Australia, contact:
Hal Leonard Australia Pty. Ltd.
4 Lentara Court
Cheltenham, Victoria, 3192 Australia
Email: info@halleonard.com.au

12

GOD ONLY KNOWS

Words and Music by JORDAN REYNOLDS,
JOEL SMALLBONE, LUKE SMALLBONE,
TEDD TJORNHOM and JOSH KERR

Moderately slow

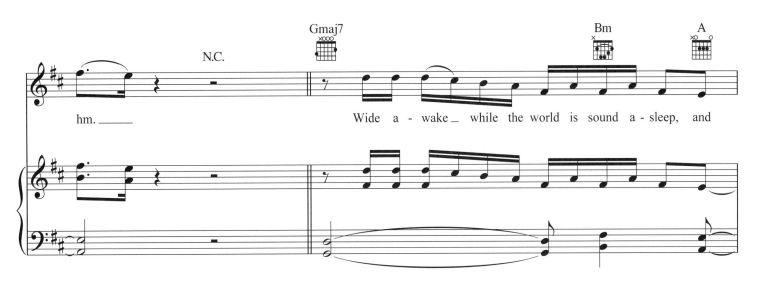

BURN THE SHIPS

Words and Music by SETH MOSLEY,
JOEL SMALLBONE, LUKE SMALLBONE
and MATT HALES

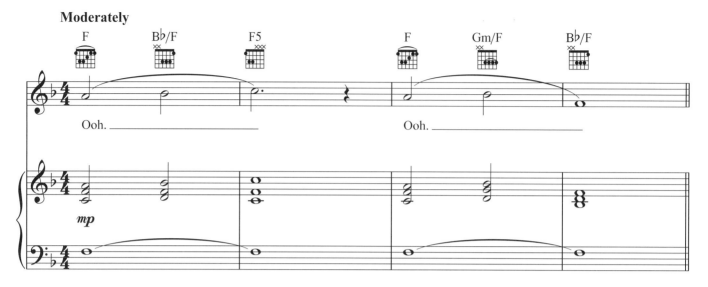

Ooh. _____ Ooh. _____

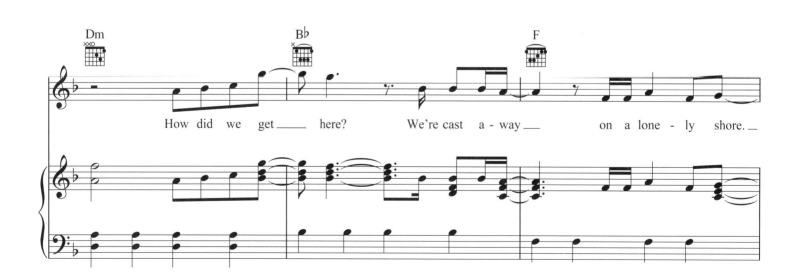

How did we get _____ here? We're cast a-way _____ on a lone-ly shore. _____

22

FAITH

Words and Music by JORDAN FELIZ,
PAUL DUNCAN and COLBY WEDGEWORTH

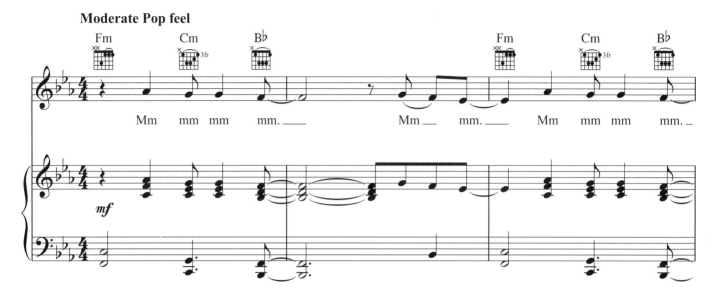

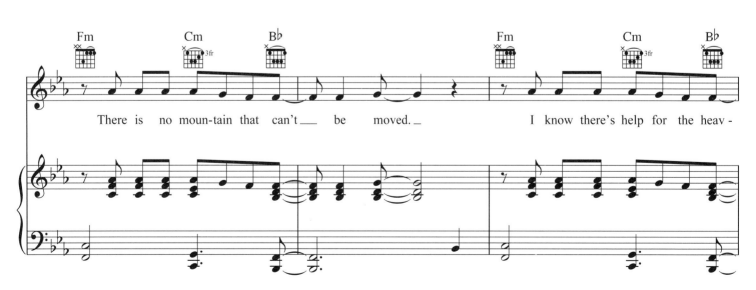

FIGHTING FOR ME

Words and Music by RILEY CLEMMONS,
JORDAN SAPP and ETHAN HULSE

Moderate Pop feel, in 2

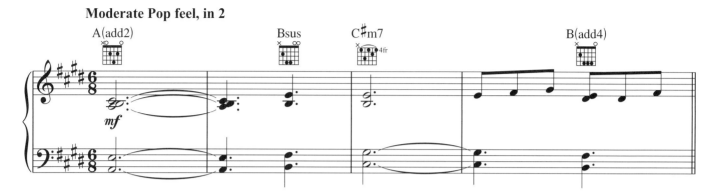

I need the kind of love that ___ can out-last the night. ___

I need the kind of love that ___ is will-ing ___ to

37

HAVEN'T SEEN IT YET

Words and Music by ETHAN HULSE,
COLBY WEDGEWORTH and DANNY GOKEY

THE GOD WHO STAYS

Words and Music by ANDREW PRUIS,
JONATHAN SMITH and MATTHEW WEST

GOD'S NOT DONE WITH YOU

Words and Music by TAUREN WELLS,
EMILY WEISBAND and BERNIE HERMS

Moderate Ballad

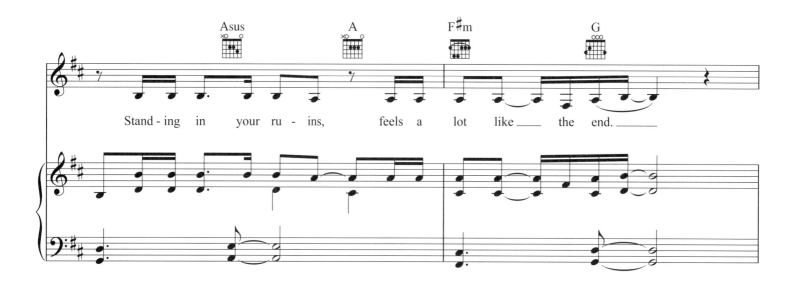

Stand-ing in your ru-ins, feels a lot like ___ the end. ___

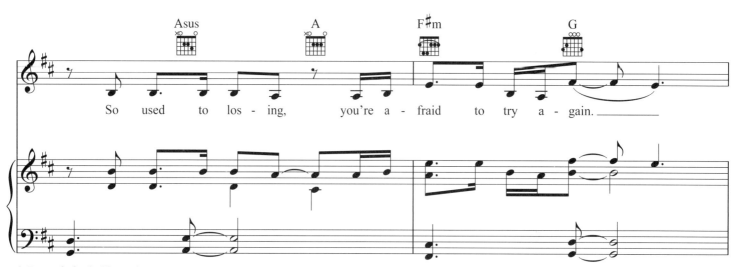

So used to los-ing, you're a-fraid to try a-gain. ___

* Recorded a half step lower.

GOOD GRACE

Words and Music by
JOEL HOUSTON

Moderately slow

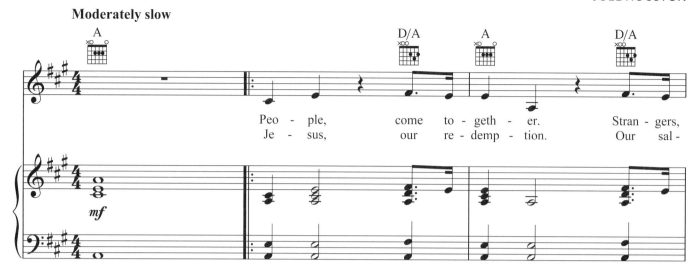

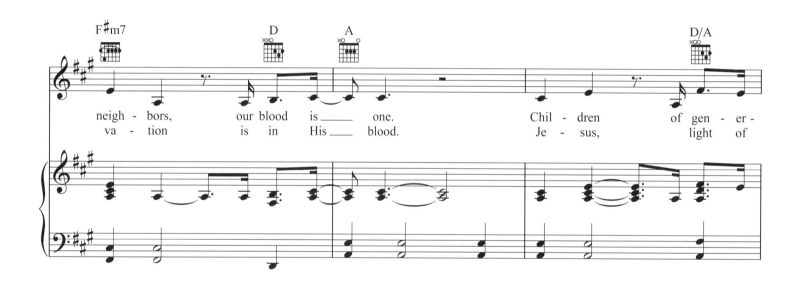

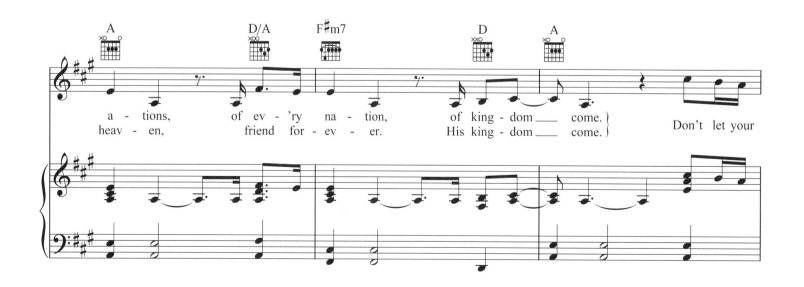

MAYBE IT'S OK

Words and Music by BRYAN FOWLER,
JONATHAN SMITH and DARREN MULLIGAN

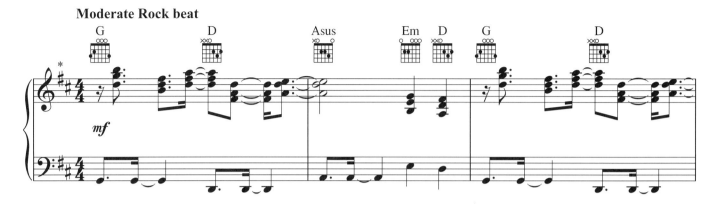

If I did-n't know ___ what it hurt like ___ to be ___ bro-
___ what it looked like ___ to be ___ dirt-

- ken, ___ then how would I know ___ what it feels like ___ to be ___ whole? ___
- y, ___ then I would-n't know ___ what it feels like ___ to be ___ clean. ___

Recorded a half step lower.

RESCUE

Words and Music by LAUREN DAIGLE,
JASON INGRAM and PAUL MABURY

Moderately slow, in 2

*You are not___ hid-den.
-tance

There's nev-er been a mo- ment___ you were for-got -ten. You are not___ hope-
that can-not be___ cov- ered___ o- ver and o- ver. You're not de-fense-

-less, though you have been___ bro- ken,___ your in-no- cence___
-less. I'll be your___ shel- ter,_____ I'll be your___

*Recorded a half step lower.

NOBODY

Words and Music by MARK HALL,
MATTHEW WEST and BERNIE HERMS

Why You ev - er

chose me has al - ways been a mys - ter - y. _____ All my life _____

_____ I've been told I be - long _____ at the end of _____ the line _____ with all the oth - er

RAISE A HALLELUJAH

Words and Music by JONATHAN DAVID HELSER,
MELISSA HELSER, MOLLY SKAGGS
and JAKE STEVENS

Moderate Rock beat

I raise a hal - le - lu - jah ____

____ in the pres-ence of my en-e-mies. ____ I

raise a hal - le - lu - jah, ____ loud - er than the un - be - lief. ____

* *Recorded a half step lower.*

REASON

Words and Music by CHAD MATTSON,
JONATHAN LOWRY and CHRIS STEVENS

Recorded a half step lower.

SCARS

Words and Music by MATTHEW ARMSTRONG,
MATTHEW HEIN, ETHAN HULSE
and JON McCONNELL

RESURRECTING

Words and Music by CHRIS BROWN,
MACK BROCK, STEVEN FURTICK,
WADE JOYE and MATTHEWS THABO NTELE

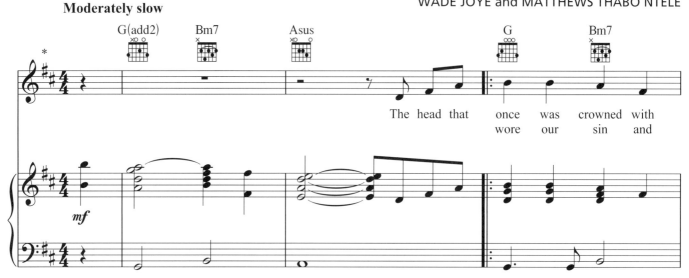

The head that once was crowned with
wore our sin and

thorns is crowned with glo - ry now. The Sav - ior
shame, now robed in maj - es - ty. The ra - di -

knelt to wash our feet; now at His feet we bow.
ance of per - fect love now shines for

Recorded a half step lower.

TILL I FOUND YOU

Words and Music by TRAVIS RYAN
and PHIL WICKHAM

Moderately slow, in 2

I searched through the earth for some-thing that could sat - is - fy, __

a peace for the hurt

I had bur-ied deep in - side. __ Knees on the floor, I

STAND IN YOUR LOVE

Words and Music by JOSH BALDWIN,
ETHAN HULSE, MARK HARRIS
and RITA SPRINGER

Moderately slow, in 2

When dark - ness tries to roll
no long - er has

o - ver my bones,
a place to hide.
when sor -
I

row comes to steal the joy I own,
am not a cap - tive to the lies.

116

YES I WILL

Words and Music by MIA FIELDES,
EDDIE HOAGLAND and JONATHAN SMITH

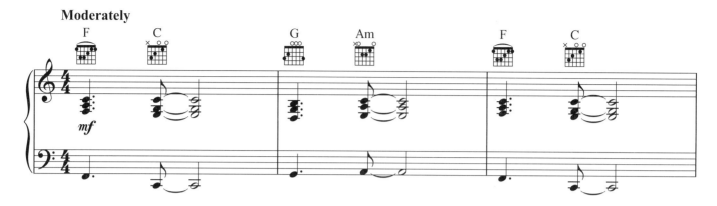

I count on one _____ thing: the same God _

_ that nev-er fails _ will not fail _ me now. ___ You won't fail _

WITH LIFTED HANDS

Words and Music by RYAN STEVENSON
and CHRIS STEVENS

GREAT CHRISTIAN COLLECTIONS FROM HAL LEONARD

51 MUST-HAVE WORSHIP CLASSICS
The title says it all! Arrangements for piano, voice, and guitar are included for the songs: Above All • As the Deer • Days of Elijah • Firm Foundation • Here I Am to Worship • In Christ Alone • Refiner's Fire • Shine, Jesus, Shine • Shout to the Lord • We All Bow Down • Your Name • and more.
00311825 P/V/G $19.99

THE BEST PRAISE & WORSHIP SONGS EVER
80 all-time favorites: Awesome God • Breathe • Days of Elijah • Here I Am to Worship • I Could Sing of Your Love Forever • Open the Eyes of My Heart • Shout to the Lord • We Bow Down • dozens more.
00311057 P/V/G $22.99

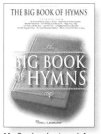

THE BIG BOOK OF HYMNS
An invaluable collection of 125 favorite hymns, including: All Hail the Power of Jesus' Name • Battle Hymn of the Republic • Blessed Assurance • For the Beauty of the Earth • Holy, Holy, Holy • It Is Well with My Soul • Just as I Am • A Mighty Fortress Is Our God • The Old Rugged Cross • Onward Christian Soldiers • Rock of Ages • Sweet By and By • What a Friend We Have in Jesus • Wondrous Love • and more.
00310510 P/V/G $22.99

CHRISTIAN CHART HITS
30 favorites from beloved Christian artists such as Kari Jobe, Jeremy Camp, Third Day, Danny Gokey, and others arranged for piano, voice and guitar. Songs include: All the People Said Amen • Blessings • Day One • Forever (We Sing Hallelujah) • Good to Be Alive • He Knows • I Need a Miracle • Lead Me • Overcomer • Tell Your Heart to Beat Again • Trust In You • We Believe • Write Your Story • You Are More • and more.
00194583 P/V/G $16.99

THE CHRISTIAN CHILDREN'S SONGBOOK
101 songs from Sunday School, all in appropriate keys for children's voices. Includes: Awesome God • The B-I-B-L-E • The Bible Tells Me So • Clap Your Hands • Day by Day • He's Got the Whole World in His Hands • I Am a C-H-R-I-S-T-I-A-N • I'm in the Lord's Army • If You're Happy and You Know It • Jesus Loves Me • Kum Ba Yah • Let There Be Peace on Earth • This Little Light of Mine • When the Saints Go Marching In • more.
00310472 P/V/G $22.99

CHRISTIAN SHEET MUSIC 2010-2019
Show your praise of God through this collection of 40 Christian favorites from the 2010s: Blessings (Laura Story) • Chain Breaker (Zach Williams) • Come to the Table (Sidewalk Prophets) • Greater (MercyMe) • Hills and Valleys (Tauren Wells) • Hope in Front of Me (Danny Gokey) • Lift My Life Up (Unspoken) • The Lion and the Lamb (Big Daddy Weave) • O' Lord (Lauren Daigle) • and more..
00345519 P/V/G $19.99

GOSPEL SONGS
Budget Books Series
Over 100 songs, including: Behold the Lamb • Down by the Riverside • Daddy Sang Bass • He Giveth More Grace • I Am Not Ashamed • In Times like These • Midnight Cry • We Are So Blessed • The Wonder of It All • and many more.
00311734 P/V/G $12.99

HILLSONG MODERN WORSHIP HITS
20 songs, including: Alive • Broken Vessels (Amazing Grace) • Christ Is Enough • Cornerstone • Forever Reign • God Is Able • Mighty to Save • Oceans (Where Feet May Fail) • The Stand • This I Believe (The Creed) • Touch the Sky • and more.
00154952 P/V/G $17.99

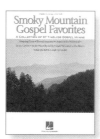

SMOKY MOUNTAIN GOSPEL FAVORITES
This collection of 37 treasured hymns includes: Amazing Grace • At the Cross • I Am Bound for the Promised Land • I Love to Tell the Story • The Old Rugged Cross • Power in the Blood • Since Jesus Came into My Heart • What a Friend We Have in Jesus • When We All Get to Heaven • and dozens more.
00310161 P/V/G $9.99

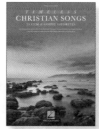

TIMELESS CHRISTIAN SONGS
A great collection of new and classic standards in Christian music, including: Amazing Grace (My Chains Are Gone) • Because He Lives • Friends • How Great Is Our God • I Can Only Imagine • Lamb of God • 10,000 Reasons (Bless the Lord) • Thy Word • and more.
00137799 P/V/G $16.99

TOP CHRISTIAN HITS OF 2019-2020
20 powerful and popular Christian songs: God Only Knows (For King and Country) • God's Not Done with You (Tauren Wells) • Haven't Seen It Yet (Danny Gokey) • Nobody (Casting Crowns) • Rescue (Lauren Daigle) • Scars (I Am They) • Till I Found You (Phil Wickham) • Yes I Will (Vertical Worship) • and more.
00334222 P/V/G $17.99

TOP 25 WORSHIP SONGS
25 contemporary worship hits are presented in this collection for piano, voice and guitar. Includes: Glorious Day (Passion) • Good, Good Father (Chris Tomlin) • Holy Spirit (Francesca Battistelli) • King of My Heart (John Mark & Sarah McMillan) • The Lion and the Lamb (Big Daddy Weave) • Reckless Love (Cory Asbury) • 10,000 Reasons (Matt Redman) • This Is Amazing Grace (Phil Wickham) • What a Beautiful Name (Hillsong Worship) • and more.
00288610 P/V/G $17.99

TRENDING WORSHIP SONGS
27 of the most popular contemporary worship songs, including: The Blessing • Build My Life • Holy Water • King of Kings • Living Hope • Nothing Else • Raise a Hallelujah • See a Victory • Way Maker • Who You Say I Am • and more.
00346008 P/V/G $17.99

25 FAVORITE WORSHIP SONGS
Worship Together Series
This matching folio features wonderful songs you know and sing, including: Amazing Grace (My Chains Are Gone) • Blessed Be Your Name • Everlasting God • Forever • Here I Am to Worship • Holy Is the Lord • How Great Is Our God • Jesus Messiah • Mighty to Save • Your Grace Is Enough • and many more.
00312123 P/V/G $16.99

THE VERY BEST OF HILLSONG
25 songs from the popular worldwide church including: Came to My Rescue • From the Inside Out • Hosanna • I Give You My Heart • Lead Me to the Cross • Mighty to Save • Shout to the Lord • The Stand • Worthy Is the Lamb • and more.
00312101 P/V/G $17.99

HAL•LEONARD®

For a complete listing of the products we have available, visit us online at halleonard.com